DEDICATION

This book contains timeless truth which I would like to dedicate to Peter Iwuoha and Immanuel Iwuoha - my children, and to the future generation.

May the wisdom embedded within its pages challenge you to be all that you can be.

Make It Happen

Alex Iwuoha

Treasure Publishing

Make It Happen

First published in the United Kingdom by
Treasure Publishing
Woodrow Business Centre
65/66 Woodrow
London SE18 5DH.

ISBN   0-9553461-0-X   978-0-9553461-0-1

Cover design and Typeset by Treasure Publishing.
www.treasurepublishing.co.uk

Printed and bound in the United Kingdom.

CONTENTS

PAGE
NUMBER

INTRODUCTION   9

1. FAILURE IS NOT FATAL   15

2. HOW DO YOU DEFINE SUCCESS?   25

3. DON'T WASTE YOUR TIME   35

4. EXCELLENCE IS MORE THAN A CLICHÉ   47

5. STINKING THINKING   57

6. YOUR ATTITUDE WILL DETERMINE
YOUR ALTITUDE   69

7. GOAL KEEPER   81

8. CHANGE YOUR BAD HABITS   93

9. CULTIVATE GOOD RELATIONSHIPS   103

10. INTEGRITY AND INTENSITY   113

11. DESIRE IS THE KEY TO MOTIVATION   123

INTRODUCTION

Some people wait

for success

to come their way,

whilst others choose to

make it happen.

If you could influence, activate or make any goal happen in the next six months, what would it be and what will you do about it?

Can you make that dream job a reality? Can you attain that desired level of qualification? Can you buy that property? Can you make that business or vision a reality? If your answer to any of these is yes, then make it happen!

Otherwise it will be a sad day when you find out that it was not accident, time or fortune that kept things from you, but yourself.

DON'T BE A WISHFUL THINKER.

The trouble with wishful thinking is that it's usually 99% wishful, 1% thinking, and 0% action. The whole essence of this book is to challenge and motivate you to bring your vision into fruition.

Wishful thinkers don't make things happen. Only those who are willing to plan, work hard and be focused end up getting to the pinnacle of their goals.

In order to make things happen, you need to have a plan and implement it. While you are doing this, things might work in your favour. But what if things work against you? Will you simply shrug your shoulders, fold your arms and surrender? If things don't work in your favour you must be determined to make progress. You must be prepared to steer your ship to your destination, even if it means you have to push against the wind. You must be willing to navigate your course to your chosen location even when there seems to be no precedent, compass or pathfinder; you must be prepared to be your own trail blazer.

STUMBLING BLOCKS

In order to make your vision happen, you might need to negotiate corners or leap over hurdles. Don't let these stumbling blocks or obstacles hinder you, make up your mind to see your dreams come true. You'll seldom find a worthwhile endeavour without stumbling blocks. Whatever you plan to achieve, hindrances will always come between you and your achievement. You can either accept them or refute them. You cannot sit on the fence.

If you really want to achieve certain goals, you cannot afford to sit back, cross your legs, twiddle your thumbs and accept things. The section in this book called Goal Keeper is dedicated to helping you achieve your goals.

BELIEVE IN YOURSELF

In order to succeed you must believe that you are capable of making things happen. This means that you must be optimistic even when others are pessimistic about you. If you don't believe in yourself, you will lack the willpower and motivation to push against obstacles.

Don't expect everyone to be excited about your vision. It is your vision and you must not allow your quest to be deflated because no one else believes in you. It is like a job search scenario. If you allow the rejection letters you receive from employers to put you off job hunting, you may never gain fulfilling employment.

The ideas set out in this book are of vital importance if you must achieve your life ambitions. They are vital for your career and will equip you with the aptitude you need to win at work, in your personal life, and in your social and business life.

To win in any area of endeavour, you must be determined to give it whatever it takes. The practical solutions proposed in this book are not about waving a magic wand. They are about giving you the tools that you need to be successful. Make good use of the tools and you will reap the dividends.

With this book I hope to keep you focused and on course. *Make It Happen* will challenge you to make a commitment towards your goals. The moment you commit yourself is when your goal is assured.

INTRODUCTION

Defeat is not failure.

Not to have tried is the true failure.

FAILURE IS NOT FATAL

Nelson Mandela spent 27 years in prison before becoming the president of South Africa. Almost 1000 banks turned down Walt Disney when he was trying to finance Disneyland. Mary Kay Ash, the billionairess founder of Mary Kay Cosmetics, sold less than £2.00 worth of cosmetics at her first beauty show.

The life experience of all these people is a strong indication that failure is not fatal. Just because you've failed does not mean you should not try again. Just because you've failed does not mean you cannot win.

WINNERS ARE NOT QUITTERS

Winners are not quitters. Quitters never end up

becoming winners. Before becoming president of the United States of America, Abraham Lincoln failed at two businesses and lost six elections. Sylvester Stallone, the American actor, was turned down time and time again when he was trying to produce his classic movie, Rocky. Thomas Edison, the American inventor, failed in almost 10,000 experiments before inventing the light bulb. He said, "I am not discouraged, because every wrong attempt discarded is another step forward." McDonalds is a big franchise today but for over a decade they introduced one poorly received sandwich after another.

These are classic examples of surviving mistakes, because the people involved accepted, learnt and moved on from their failures. They understood that if you want to win, you must not quit. They seemed to epitomised the words of the Irish novelist James Joyce, "Mistakes are the portals of discovery."

PEOPLE KEEP CHANGING THE DEFINITION OF FAILURE

People erroneously conclude that you are a failure when you lack success in an endeavour. If people notice that you've made several unsuccessful attempts they consider you a failure. But, you must not allow people's definition of failure to affect you.

At one time, if you were tall and slim you were considered good looking. At another time "they" said, "you need to be big". Some time ago, one of the tests of masculinity was a man's ability to hold back tears. Today, a man weeping in public is acceptable, and as a result sports stars all over the world are eager to shed a few tears when they lose a sports game.

People always change their opinions, likewise their definitions and yardsticks. That's why different styles of dressing come in and go out of fashion. Just as soon as you try to catch up with the latest fashion in vogue, there is a new trend in the market. So you must conclude that you are not a failure simply because people say so, but only if you give up the desire to succeed.

TRIED AND FAILED IS BETTER THAN FAILED TO TRY

Someone can become so afraid of failure that they never attempt to try. If you tried and failed, that is an achievement. You have tried. No one can take that from you. But if you fail to try, what is your achievement? Nothing! Because you have failed to try.

Most successful business men and women would tell you they've tried and failed many times and have learnt from their mistakes. Most Olympic gold medalists have experienced several unsuccessful attempts before they finally reached the pinnacle of their goals. The majority of drivers did not pass their first driving test.

Who then can you classify as a failure? Could it be the person who tried several times and eventually succeeds or the person who is too afraid to try?

Henry Ford, the American industrialist who started the Ford Motor Company, taught his workers, "Failure is the opportunity to begin again more intelligently." Second business attempts succeed far more often because you have the benefit of hindsight and you're more experienced than the first time.

If you keep trying and keep learning, you put the odds for success in your favour. American inventor Thomas Edison said, "Many of life's failures are people who did not realize how close they were to success when they gave up."

YOU LEARN TO TALK BY STUTTERING

The first few times you tried to talk, you stuttered. Did stammering make you stop talking when you were a child? Oh no, you waffled your way through until you were able to communicate. The first time you tried to walk, you staggered and fell down. Did you give up? No. You got up and tried again.

You may not remember the first few times you tried to dress yourself. You probably looked like a clown with a left foot in the right shoe and vice versa. Your buttons were probably done in no particular order but it did not matter if they were out of sequence. If anyone told you that you were not properly dressed it did not hinder you from trying again.

Learning to drive a car may not have been all that easy for you either. So why would you think that you couldn't make it in life just because you failed a few times? Don't be afraid of failure, because the fear of failure can so often overwhelm a desire to succeed.

Many people fail because they quit too soon. They lose faith when the signs are against them. They do not have the courage to hold on and to keep fighting in spite of that which seems insurmountable. If more of us would strike out and attempt the "impossible," we would achieve the "unachievable."

THINGS THAT HURT... INSTRUCT

The mistakes you've made and bad experiences you've had should all culminate into one thing: Instruction.

Don't feel too bad about things that hurt you but learn from them. Let your mistakes be a springboard that would catapult you to your goals. When you fail an exam, you ought to be disappointed, and something else you ought to do is to be determined to pass the exam next time. Remember that any exam or test is meant to confirm what you know and reveal things you don't know. Likewise when you fail a driving test, you are exposed to your flaws. To pass the test next time you must learn from your faults.

Life sometimes breaks us, but when we heal, we're stronger in the parts that once were broken. If you've ever experienced failure in a business endeavour, you should review your strategy, identify your strengths and weaknesses, and how not to do business next time. Unfortunately people experience failure in business and become too scared to try again. If you've experienced marriage failure, it should not deter you from getting married again, but let it motivate you to aim for a successful marriage next time. Let things that hurt you, instruct you.

POOR EDUCATION SHOULD NOT
HINDER A RICH FUTURE

- Winston Churchill, the British Prime Minister, graduated last in his college class.

- Muriel Seibert was the first woman to make one billion dollars and she only had a high school diploma.

- Richard Branson, the British founder of Virgin Airlines, with a net worth of over £3.5 billion, dropped out of high school.

- Steven Spielberg, the American film director, was an unknown C student in high school.

- Thomas Edison, the man who invented the light bulb had only three months of formal education.

- Sean Connery, the James Bond actor, quit school at age 13 with a sixth grade education. One of his early jobs was polishing coffins. His first acting coach told him that he needed more education. Thereafter he started educating himself.

- Henry Ford accumulated a fortune, not because of his superior mind, but because he overlooked temporary defeats, which he had to surmount before striking it rich in the automobile industry.

Although these people had a poor start, they did not end up poor. Their lives started with little education, but ended up with a wealth of experience, skills and knowledge. Little education ought not to be a barrier to a rich future.

FAILURE IS NOT BITTER IF YOU DO NOT SWALLOW IT

If you don't understand failure, it will undermine you. Although a failure feels like forever, it is fleeting. We all must graduate from the school of failure in order to gain entrance into the University of Success.

Failure does not stand in the way; it is the way. People seldom begin as a success: Failure is the polish that enables the success in us to shine. By learning how to take advantage of failure you learn how to succeed. Here are some thoughts on failures:

- **They are only lessons.** Every event in the universe offers a teaching. Look for the lesson and you can then pass the grade. There are no failures, only lessons.

- **Failures teach success.** Every failure is the step to success if you take it that way. By learning how not to fail you are automatically learning more about how to succeed. Every failure is a potential lesson in success.

- **Failures are not "bad".** Nothing is inherently "bad" or "good". It's what you do with something that makes it so. If you take it that failure is "bad," then it could be bad, but if you look for the good news in every failure; it becomes good.

- **Failures can be "good".** Every event in the universe can be helpful. Defeat can make you stand up on your feet; endings make way for beginnings; the worst trial can set you free. Make your failures work for you, not against you.

- **Failures are not final.** Failure is not the same thing as falling down. Even if you fall down, it is staying down that incapacitates you. But then, all you are doing is learning another lesson. Perhaps the ultimate lesson is that you are always learning from past mistakes and are willing to give yourself another chance.

Tomorrow's success is determined by how you handle the failures of yesterday and today. Just keep in mind that when your plans fail… it is a temporary defeat and not a permanent failure. Remember, failure is not fatal.

Birds sing after a storm.

Why shouldn't we?

Better to deal with the

problems of success

than the stagnation of failure.

HOW DO YOU DEFINE SUCCESS?

According to Ralph Waldo Emerson, the definition of success is "to laugh much; to win respect of intelligent persons and the affections of children; to earn the approbation of honest critics and endure the betrayal of false friends; to appreciate beauty; to find the best in others; to give oneself; to leave the world a little better, whether by a healthy child, a garden patch, or a redeemed social condition; to have played and laughed with enthusiasm, and sung with exultation; to know even one life has breathed easier because you have lived - this is to have succeeded."

That was Ralph's definition, but what is your definition of success? Let's start the definition and discussion of success with some self assessment questions. First question: Would you rather be a big fish in a small pond or a small fish in a big pond?

Let's ponder on this question for a second: A big fish might consider itself successful because it is big and a major force to reckon with in a small pond, and a small fish might consider itself successful because it is in a big pond and has lots of potential for growth and expansion. Which would you rather be?

Another question: Would you prefer to be a successful head of a middle-management team or a flawed and unsuccessful CEO of a major world-wide conglomerate? One more question: Would you prefer a lavish size, luxurious office in a prestigious building in the heart of the city with a low income, or a little desk, a petite office, in an insignificant area outside the city, but with a much higher income?

The truth is many people often choose to have the trappings of success rather than actual success. As long as the old adage "one man's meat is another man's poison" is still relevant, success will always have a different meaning to everyone. But, I will rather define success as winning instead of appearing to be winning. Success means investing in the future rather than borrowing from your future. At the end of a work day, success means completing few tasks rather than having a long list of uncompleted tasks.

THE SECRETS TO SUCCESS

The secrets to success are not a secret. It takes more than having the right information; it takes tenacity, commitment and determination to become successful. So there is no secret to success.

If you want to be successful in a chosen field, find the people who have achieved commendable results in the field. Study their lifestyle and management style. Enquire about how they have dealt with issues and difficult situations. This way you will learn from the experience of others. If no one has ever gone down the route you plan to take, you can benchmark it with other successful ventures albeit in a different field, and let their achievements encourage and motivate you to become successful in your own unique venture.

According to Theodore Roosevelt, an American President in the early 20th Century, "There are two kinds of success. One is the very rare kind that comes to the man who has the power to do what no one else has the power to do. That is genius. But the average man who wins what we call success is not a genius. He is a man who has merely the ordinary qualities that he shares with his fellows, but who has developed those ordinary qualities to a more than ordinary degree."

PAY THE PRICE

If you really want to succeed you can, but you must be willing to develop your ordinary qualities. In other words, you must pay the right price. Success doesn't come cheap, although it may appear cheap to people after they've seen you become successful. People always see the glory but they don't know the story.

If you are willing to make sacrifices and give it all it takes, then you are most likely to succeed. If you have the desire to succeed at anything, I will suggest that you look at three things:

■ Your need
■ Your ability
■ Your willingness

First, list the things you **need** to do in order to achieve your aim; secondly, list those things you are **able** to do and thirdly, things you are **willing** to do in order to achieve your goal. This is how you count the cost of success in order to decide if you can and want to pay the price.

DO YOUR HOMEWORK

Whatever your field of endeavour, if you want to succeed you must do your homework. From sales to tendering for contract, from a desire to run a successful conference to a quest to be successful at an interview, homework is vital.

Preparation, rehearsal, research and planning are essential if you want to succeed. Use the internet, your local library, and telephone to gather as much information as possible. Thereafter, do your rehearsals. Have a private rehearsal before you do a public presentation. Do your homework before you leave home for a job interview, practice your presentation before you get to the meeting and decide how you would like to close the deal before you make the telephone call. Anticipate challenges and difficulties and plan for a way out.

True success spends a lot of time in preparation. Military strategists will tell you that the time spent on reconnaissance is rarely wasted. An entrepreneur will tell you that a business plan is always an eye opener.

LOOK BEFORE YOU LEAP

Another difference between successful and unsuccessful people is that the former would do a job and check it again and again before making a presentation, whilst the latter is too eager to make a presentation and reluctant to check the work again.

A popular saying with workmen is – "measure twice, cut once". Before you make a presentation take another look at your checklist, before you deliver, glance once again at your delivery note. Always ensure that you are satisfied before you wrap up a project.

YOU MUST BE DECISIVE

Unless you take action, nothing happens. If you want to be successful you must be decisive. You must not pro-crastinate. You should not be complacent and sit around waiting for things to happen.

If you want to learn how to do something, begin. That's why Nike - the sports garment company's slogan is "Just Do It!" The beginning is the most important part of any work. You don't stand a chance if you don't start. John Maxwell, the American motivational speaker said, "Successful people make important decisions early in life and manage those decisions for the rest of their lives."

Even though it is important that you are decisive, you must also be flexible, versatile and ready to adapt as and when needed. Successful people choose the best option and don't look back. They have self-confidence, are bold and do what must be done. When something is wrong and it's your business, take action to make it right. Don't look for excuses or who to place the blame on. If you do, you will keep looking for people to validate your excuses. Review the facts and consider your options.

IS YOUR BEST GOOD ENOUGH?

In any game of sports, only the best team wins the trophy, not every participating team. Olympic gold medalists are rewarded not just because they showed up at the games, but because they are the final winners. At your place of employment, you are offered a job, not just because you attended an interview, but because you seemed to be the best person for the job. Employers don't pay their staff merely because they show up at work; remuneration is a reward for carrying out your duties. You get paid a salary because you get the job done.

If you are a business person, you will realise that your customers don't reward you because you tried hard to deliver. You enjoy the patronage of your customers because of your positive results.

Don't give yourself a pat on the back because you are try-ing your best. Ask yourself - is your best good enough?

Efforts are good, but positive outcomes are better. Trying hard is nice, but meeting targets is nicer. Hard work is not bad, but maximum output is great. Starting a deal is merely a beginning, but closing the deal is the conclusion of the transaction.

Whatever your field of endeavour, be it at work, school, business or family, don't settle for average efforts or mere attendance. You get rewarded for results not efforts.

Great successes are built on taking your negatives and turning them around.

It's the little things

that make the

big things possible.

DON'T WASTE YOUR TIME

This section will give you some hints on how to recognise and prune the non-productive, time-wasting activities in your life and consolidate your time for important tasks.

Time is measured in seconds, minutes, hours, days, weeks, months and years. If you are prone to wasting your seconds and minutes, you will most likely squander your months and years.

After a game, a professional football coach said: "We didn't lose the game; we just ran out of time." But if the truth be told, if you don't win a game within the set time, you'll end up losing the game. The proper use of time affects your success or failure. That is why it is important not to waste your valuable time. You can do this by doing more with less time, by achieving tomorrow's target today and by investing your time today in a venture that will achieve dividends tomorrow.

LATE AND LACKADAISICAL

Have you heard of the joke: "He'll be late to his own funeral?" People who are habitual latecomers would be late to any function irrespective of what others do to help them come early. In the UK, the clock goes forward by one hour just before the summer to give people an hour's head start, yet some people still arrive late for their appointments. People turn up late for engagements even when they set their watches five minutes ahead. They are late for work even if they wake up early.

There appear to be two groups of people. Those who have a good sense of timing and are planners - generally prepared for most contingencies - and those who tend to run late for just about everything and have to rush at the last minute to get things done.

CHRONIC LATENESS

When latecomers graduate to become chronic latecomers, people might refer to them as "time thieves". This is someone who has questionable and even faulty conceptions of time commitments, scheduling and time management. Many people in this category think nothing of being late.

Differences in pace often have their roots in deeply ingrained habits and attitudes of a specific culture itself. Certain cultures appear to be chronically laid back and late. Others, such as those in big cities where everything runs to tight schedules, are usually "time aware."

Time thieves are people who say, "Why do it today, when we can do it tomorrow?" When they need things they say, "I needed it yesterday." Time conscious people plan ahead and say, "I finished it yesterday!"

Some people enjoy the adrenaline rush of cutting things close to deadlines. Chronically late people apologise and feel guilt-free when keeping others waiting. Yet, every time they are late, they are causing anxiety for others. They do not know how to coordinate their time or tend to over-extend themselves, committing to more things than they can handle. They underestimate how much time things take to complete.

Such people do not care if they are late. They expect the world to understand that they are busy or that this is their pattern. Actually, this group of people generally have a pattern of their own when it comes to being late. They are often 30 minutes or one hour late so those who are on-time adjust and invite them one hour earlier to make up for their lateness.

In most things we do in life - we have obstacles and delays - things go wrong. One must factor these into the equation when planning any project. Things change and the end result will vary from that which was originally planned.

THE SOLUTION FOR LATENESS

Are you a chronic latecomer? Examine your patterns to find out why. There are endless excuses for chronic lateness but few good reasons. If you want to correct this pattern, you will find the concise, clear and usable recommendations in this book very helpful.

I.   HAVE A PLAN

Time is a precious commodity which needs to be properly managed. The first step toward effective time-management is to have a plan for each day. In other words have a to-do list.

Quite often, people cram their day with a list of things to do, which are merely wishful thoughts rather than things they can actually do. If you want to be a person of integrity, you must be careful to differentiate what you can do from what you would like to do.

It is better to have a few things that you can actually do than a long list that you cannot finish. It is better to have five things on your daily "to do list" and enjoy the satisfaction of accomplishing all your tasks than to have 20 things and only manage to get two done. Be realistic - don't be too ambitious but write down what you hope to achieve on a daily basis. This is one way to make good use of your time.

2.   TIME YOUR PLAN

Another helpful thing to do is to earmark time towards each activity on your things-to-do list. If you don't allocate start and finish times to your daily agenda, you'll probably misappropriate a lot of your precious time. Golda Mier, the former Israeli Prime Minister, who accomplished so much for peace in the Middle East, said "I must govern the clock, not be governed by it."

Remember that many things can go wrong even when you time your plan. So do what building contractors do; add contingency time just in case things don't go according to plan. Building contractors often add 25 to 50 percent to the time they think a task will take. For example if you estimate that it will take 30 minutes to get to that job interview, allow 45 minutes. You may prefer the peace instead of the adrenalin rush.

Traffic situations can be sometimes unpredictable. All it takes is bad weather, an accident, a burst pipe or something else to bring traffic to a halt. If you add contingency time, you can relax knowing that if there is unexpected traffic you can still make it to your destination on time.

Traffic on most roads have peaks and troughs. During rush hours, roads leading to city or town centres are often very busy. If you cannot avoid traveling during rush hour, allow more time than usual for your travel.

If there is some construction work being undertaken, the traffic tends to build up. You may want to avoid road construction routes and if you can't, allow plenty of extra time.

3.   *MAKE QUALITY USE OF YOUR SPARE TIME*
Can you think of any unproductive things you do on a daily basis? If yes, you should consider weeding them out. If you chat and banter for too long on the telephone, watch too much television and hang around people who

have plenty of time and don't care how they use it, you are squandering your time. Dr. Martin Luther King, the American civil rights activist, said, "The time is always right to do what is right."

If the phone rings just as you're leaving your home or office, let your answering machine take the call... Unless you are expecting someone to call about the current item on your agenda – your destination. If the call is not about the destination you're about to leave for, that message can probably wait until later on. It will still be waiting for you on your answering machine when you return. Make no mistake about it, if you pick up that phone, you will be late!

Many day-to-day needs can be taken care of in your spare time and when you are not desperate. For example, always make sure you have enough petrol in the car. Go to the ATM or bank and get the spare cash you'll need. Put your briefcase, purse or wallet right near the door. Gather what you're going to wear, so you can simply grab everything and get dressed quickly. You'll save lots of pre-cious time if you do the things that are not urgent ahead of when they are needed.

If you have to get your children ready for school in the morning, do the same for them: Make sure all of their belongings are prepared the night before. Be sure they'll wake up in good time to get dressed and have breakfast.

4.   GET A GOOD NIGHT'S SLEEP

A good night's sleep is an advantage to you. Don't get into the bad habit of giving up your sleep time. You will find some people who claim to get only 3-5 hours of sleep per night. Some stay awake all night watching television until 4.00 am instead of getting a good night sleep. Sleeping is restorative. For the majority of people, getting less than 7-8 hours of sleep will do them a disservice. Sleep deprivation can mess up your day. It can make you weak and unproductive.

5.   PLAN AND REVIEW

Plan your day before the day, likewise your route before you travel. If you're not really sure how to get to your destination, allow for extra time. If possible, drive to that destination prior to your appointment. This way, you'll know exactly how to get there on your scheduled day. If that isn't possible, call someone at your destination. Ask for specific directions and write them down. You can also use a map service on the internet.

In addition to your route, you need to plan your daily activities. With the aid of a Day Planner you'll find out the right pace for your body, mind, and soul.

Finally, review the day's activities at the end of each day. It is always productive to evaluate how you've spent your day. This will help you establish the things you gave too much or too little time to. Evaluation always gives you insight into areas that need correction.

STOP WASTING YOUR TIME

You can learn from the American statesman, Benjamin Franklin who said, "Lost time is never found again," and the Victorian English author, Charles Dickens who warned that, "Procrastination is the thief of time."

Value your time. Spend it doing what you want to do. Delegate other jobs so that you can concentrate on higher priority tasks. There are a lot of people, places and things competing for your time. You should be in control of it and learn to say no to invitations or requests that will squander your time.

Discourage people from just dropping in and interrupting your work. If you have a secretary or assistant, they can take messages and arrange appointments for you. Voicemail and email can help you protect your work time. Be sure that you have the skills, time and resources to complete requests before accepting them and allowing them to interfere with current projects.

COMMON TIME WASTERS

Here are a few typical time wasters to guard against:

- Not planning or poor planning
- Lack of self-discipline
- Not prioritising tasks
- Mistakes
- Pointless meetings
- Perfectionism
- Poor communication
- Equipment failure
- Socialising during work time
- Inability to say "No"
- Inability to make decisions
- Inability to delegate
- Lack of motivation or interest
- Procrastination

Isn't it strange that some people complain that they don't have enough time to get things done, yet they find enough time to do nothing?

DON'T WASTE YOUR TIME

Only close attention

to the fine details of

any operation makes the

operation first-class

EXCELLENCE IS MORE THAN A CLICHÉ

There was a time, when I was responsible for a team of volunteers that produces a church's weekly bulletin. I made it a rule that no weekly bulletin should ever be published until it was as near perfection as human care and skill could make it.

I told the team, "God needs the bulletin to send his message across to the congregation, and if the bulletin has mistakes, God's message could be misrepresented."

Would you be bold enough to make this kind of statement about the things you do? Could you honestly say that you do your best at your voluntary or paid work?

Excellence is not about being perfect. You are a man or woman of excellence not because you have no flaws, but because you excel. You achieve excellence because you've attained a level that is higher than your previous. In other words, you exceed your last level of achievement. Excellence is not about being a perfectionist and fussing endlessly over meaningless details. Excellence is about making daily, gradual progress in improving your standards and quality. It is a state of surpassing merit or quality in a service or product.

Find your personal best and work to this level. Pride yourself on breaking your last records and you will find that everyone who meets and deals with you will benefit from your commitment to being your best.

You should have a principle of always aiming for excellence. Make it a core value from which you do not waver.

THE STUDY OF EXCELLENCE

Excellence is a common word in mission statements. Many organisations claim to aim for excellence, but excellence is more than a mere cliché. That is why many so-called "excellent" organisations in the past have since fallen from grace. The formula for their success in the past were no longer relevant for their future. Only a dynamic and learning organisation can claim excellence.

In their study of 62 successful American companies, *In Search of Excellence* (Harper Collins Publishers, Inc), documented in their book, the authors, Tom Peters and Robert Waterman identified the following eight basic attributes of excellence:

1. *A bias for action* – being action oriented and with a bias for getting things done.
2. *Close to the customer* – listening and learning from the people they serve and providing quality, service and reliability.
3. *Autonomy and entrepreneurship* – innovation and risk-taking as an expected way of doing things.
4. *Productivity through people* – treating members of staff as the source of quality and productivity.
5. *Hands-on, value driven* – having well defined basic philosophies and top management keeping in touch with the people in the front lines.
6. *Stick to the knitting* – staying close to what they know and can do well.
7. *Simple form, lean staff* – simple structural forms and systems and few top level staff.

8. *Simultaneous loose-tight properties* – operational decentralisation but strong centralised control over the few, important core values.

A key factor in organisational effectiveness is the successful management of change and innovation. Any organisation that refuses to embrace change cannot claim to be an organisation of excellence. In fact, those who chose to stick with the ways in which they have always managed won't be around to witness their own defeat. They, and their organisations, would become footnotes in history after a while.

MAXIMISE YOUR STRENGTHS

Excellence is about being open to new ideas and new ways of doing things, but it does not mean you must always abandon your winning formula. Don't change a winning team just for the sake of change.

Every individual and organisation has strengths and weaknesses. If you must make a choice between maximising your strengths and minimising your weaknesses, what would you choose? If you must decide whether to stick to what you know how to do and learn what you don't know, which would you rather go for? It is like a vehicle in motion; it is easier to steer and push a vehicle which is already in motion than to get a stalled vehicle to move. Therefore, make good use of your strengths; invest in improving your strengths instead of your weaknesses.

In order to maximise your strengths you must be willing to go beyond average. You must aim to be the best. Think about it, how fast can a cheetah run? How tall can a tree be? How strong can a lion be? How loud can a cock crow? The answers are - as fast as possible, as tall as possible, as strong as possible and as loud as possible. Aim to be limitless. If nothing is in your way, don't hinder your achievements. Even where there are obstacles in the way, aim to overcome them and be all you can be.

WORK SMARTER, NOT HARDER

A person of excellence is a person who knows how to work smarter, not necessarily harder. This book is unequivocally in support of hard work. I espouse inspiration, but I also support perspiration alongside inspiration, because you get more inspired to do something - when you start doing it.

Someone once said "It always takes less time to do something right than to do it over." Overall, I would rather aim to work smarter than to work harder. I would rather try to get more results with lesser efforts than to put in more efforts in order to get more results. If you can devise a strategy or make use of a tool in order to attain a better output, go ahead and make full use of it.

Hard work is good, but smart work is better although there will be busy times when you may need to do extra hours of work, especially at the start of a new project. Nurse it and give it all it takes to achieve long term sustainability. However it doesn't make much sense burning out through 70 hours working week for an unhealthy period of time. Most millionaires only work between 40 to 50 hours a week. What makes the difference is to actually enjoy the work you do. Don't do a job you hate, or you'll be less creative and successful.

Smart work is better than hard work. It is about achieving more with less. Rather than increasing your input in order to achieve more output, find a way, strategy or tool to help you achieve maximum output with minimum input.

This is why businesses engage in synergic relationships, so that 1 + 1 are no longer equal to 2, but 3 or more. Synergy helps businesses to achieve more with less.

MAKE A DIFFERENCE

If you are not making a difference with your life, it doesn't matter how long it is. Life should be measured, not in terms of its duration, but in terms of its donation.

People are not remembered for how long they live but how well. Long life is good but a quality life is better. Therefore, whatever you do, make a difference. You'll become more effective and productive if you decide that the things you do will make a difference.

You may not be able to make a difference on the world stage, but you can make a difference in your own world. You may not be able to make a difference in your organisation but you may be able to play a major role in your department. You may not be able to change your nation or city, but you can be influential in your home. Whoever coined the expression "charity begins at home," must have had this section of this book in mind. Whatever you do, make a decision to do it very well.

Once upon a time, a man and his son were taking a stroll along the seashore when the man noticed some starfish which were washed ashore. His son watched in surprise as his father picked up one fish after another and threw them back into the sea. The son said, "But Dad, why are you throwing the starfish back into the sea? It doesn't make any difference as there are many of them on the seashore." The father picked up another fish and said, "Son, to this particular fish, I have made a difference" and tossed it into the river. "I may not be able to save all the fish on the river bank, but I have saved this one."

If you aim to make a difference and you are determined to be the best at whatever you do, you will be influential, and you will become a person of excellence.

You are doing your best

only when you are trying to

improve what you are doing.

As you think,

so you are.

STINKING THINKING

The smell of a rose reminds us of the visual appearance of a rose. What you smell, see, hear, taste or touch affects what you perceive in your mind, and this affects what you say and do. If you always accommodate negative thinking, you will be a pessimistic person. So if you want to achieve positive results in any area of life you should get rid of negative thoughts and be willing to embrace positive and optimistic thoughts about your intent.

CONTROL YOUR NEGATIVE THOUGHTS

Your thought patterns can impair your ability to take appropriate action irrespective of the truth about the situation. They can be self-defeating and distort the reality of the world around you. There are various types of negative thoughts, but let's discuss three main types: 1) Negative thoughts about yourself; 2) Negative thoughts about others; and 3) Negative thoughts about the future.

Let's look at each of these types of negative thinking a little more closely:

1.   NEGATIVE THOUGHTS ABOUT YOURSELF

Negative thoughts about yourself are usually self-criticisms which tend to be absolute, such as, "I'm worthless" or, "I am no good." Negative thoughts can emanate from negative experiences or fear of failure. It is okay to reprimand yourself if you make mistakes, but it becomes counter productive if you are perpetually pessimistic about your potential or capability due to past failures.

2.   NEGATIVE THOUGHTS ABOUT OTHERS

Cynicism is another name for negative thinking about others. Cynical people are sarcastic and they often doubt, distrust and are suspicious of others. Even when others are kind, helpful or generous they are always looking out for ulterior motives. Cynical people generalise the bad experiences they've had with a few people and see most people in a negative light.

3.   NEGATIVE THOUGHTS ABOUT THE FUTURE

Another type of negative thinking is hopelessness about the future. If you are hopeless about your future you will lack the willpower to try to improve it. These thoughts mislead a person into resigning to fate. It is a fatalistic way of thinking which is far worse than pessimistic thinking.

Your thought patterns affect your actions. If you want to act positively you should be willing to think positively.

STOP THE BLAME CULTURE

When you plant a potato and it does not grow well, you don't blame the potato. You look for the reasons why it is not doing well: It may need fertilizer, more water or less sun but you would rarely blame the potato. Yet when we have problems at work, with friends or family, we tend to blame the other party.   Instead, we should learn how to take care of them and the relationships will grow well like healthy potatoes. Blaming has no positive effect at all, the important point is to try to understand and make every effort to change the situation.

Whenever you want to complain about a fault, it would be more helpful to add a suggestion on how to correct the fault. Mere complaining or blame does not often lead to correction. Rather it may lead to resistance or defiance.

Sometimes your complaint may be justified. However, much complaining is pointless and only adds to the frustration. Complaint by itself is meaningless unless it is followed with a suggestion. Start making suggestions rather than complaints; this is how to make things happen.

YOUR ENVIRONMENT CAN AFFECT YOUR THOUGHTS

The environment in which you live can affect what you believe and achieve.

If a child lives in a home where they are always rebuked and reprimanded, the child will grow up with low self esteem. If a child lives in a home or environment where they are always appreciated or celebrated, the child will have confidence and empowerment to believe in him or herself. A child who lives in a hostile environment will learn to be violent. A child who lives with ridicule tends to become shy. A child who lives with shame learns to feel guilty.

Just as an environment can affect the future of a child, an adult's environment equally influences their thought pattern. If you can do anything about your environment, choose to hang around people who can positively influence your mind. That's why you must choose your friends carefully, and you must also be very selective about your mentors. You should not be a friend to someone just because they want you to be their friend.

If you are not careful you could be trapped in someone else's negative thinking. You should have progressive and positive-minded friends. Hang around people who are thinking about progress and aiming to improve their lives. If you choose the wrong set of friends and spend sufficient time with them, you will begin to share in their negative thinking. Remember the saying "birds of the same feather flock together."

YOUR HAPPINESS DEPENDS ON YOU

You can become the master of your moods. You can't always control what happens to you, but you can control what happens inside you, and how you respond to your moods. Happiness is a choice. Many years ago, Aristotle said, "Happiness depends upon ourselves."

You can choose to be happy on any occasion irrespective of any unforeseen circumstances. It doesn't matter if it rains, snows or if the sun shines on the day you have a major event, you can choose to be happy. Your happiness depends entirely on you. If it rains on your special event or occasion such as your wedding day or a major outdoor show, you may not like it but you can choose to control your temper and your mood.

When you are under pressure your disposition is entirely your choice. You can remain calm under pressure or infect everyone around you with the anxiety and strain of your pressure. Your frame of mind depends on you. When you are happy, it affects your creativity. That is why success is often linked with happiness. Former US President Franklin Roosevelt said, "Men are not prisoners of fate, but only prisoners of their own minds."

LOOK OUT FOR POSITIVE LESSONS IN NEGATIVE SITUATIONS

If you seek, you will find. People tend to find what they are looking for. If you want to review your performance and all you look out for are weaknesses, you may not see the good side of your performance. It is also important to consider the positive side of things such as your strengths.

SWOT (Strengths, Weaknesses, Opportunities and Threats) is a major tool for analysing the strategic advantage of an organisation or event. This SWOT analysis provides convenient headings under which to study an organisation, event or situation, and may provide a basis for decision-making and problem–solving.

It is widely accepted that corporate performance is influenced by a combination of internal and external factors. These factors can be characterised as the organisation's "strengths" and "weaknesses" and its external "opportunities" and "threats".

If you concentrate on the bad (what didn't work, what isn't beautiful and what you dislike) that's what you'll find. If you consciously look out for the good, you will find much more to smile about. Likewise, if you want to see the good in people you have to stop focusing on their mistakes and pay attention to their strengths.

Be careful how you interpret negative events. You should view negative events in such a way that is less damaging to your self-confidence and sustains your hope and trust in other people.

If you look out for the positive in any negative situation you will become an optimist. Optimists are always hopeful and confident. Even when they fail, they utilise failure as a course of correction.

BE OPEN TO CRITICISM

Many people find it difficult to accept criticism and will immediately assume a defensive attitude intent on counterattacking. They only listen to hear for an opening so that they can strike back. Such people seldom learn from their mistakes. Sometimes, people will misunderstand or misjudge you. If someone makes a wrong assessment of your actions, don't get angry and strike back. You cannot stop what they think but be open to criticism and look at the incident as an opportunity for improvement.

When you are criticised you may respond in one of the following ways: Retaliate - "an eye for an eye". At other times you become defensive by giving the critique "the edge of your tongue" or you can be receptive and thank the offender for presenting you with this opportunity to be the master of your emotions. Of course, being human and imperfect, you accept that a critical evaluation of your efforts may be justified. Listen for constructive criticism. You may learn of mistakes that you can correct. You may learn of important steps that you may have skipped. You may learn of alternative strategies, perspectives, ideas and theories. To get rid of "stinking thinking" you must be willing to accept criticism.

THE INCREDIBLE POWER OF THE MIND

Although the mind is mentioned last in this chapter, it comes first in the order of importance because it is the centre for your emotions and decisions.

Neurons in the brain generate the initial electrical signals to do work, but the instructions to generate those electrical signals come from the mind. Although the brain and the mind are separate, they are linked. The mind is a place - a dynamic environment - within your body. It is the invisible headquarters where decisions are made. In the mind resides the quiet spiritual observer. The brain is simply the link between the invisible and material – it might interest you to know that each human being is a spirit which has a soul and lives in a body.

When people speak of the mind and the body they often refer to them as things they own - "my body," "my mind". You are neither your mind, nor your body; they are simply things you possess during your physical life here on earth. As a result, they are tools and you may use them as you desire.

Because the mind is linked to the brain, it is possible to use your mind to signal the brain to activate these neurons and then for the brain to prepare the body for work. That's why you must visualise or have a blue print of something before you do it. Visualisation is a form of mental programming whereby the desired result is achieved in the inner world - the mind.

The power of the human mind should not be understated or misunderstood. Many times people program themselves for success, or failure. For instance, a person who had never played table tennis in his life was challenged by a friend to play a game. The man remarked, "I have never played in my life. I can't play. I will lose the game if I play."

After being convinced to play, the man picked up a bat and ball, played and missed and remarked, "See? I told you I am useless at table tennis." What can be gleaned from his statements? First, the man stated that he was "useless" - before he even tried. Thus, in his mind he created an expectation - a belief - of how reality in the physical would turn out.

In his mind he had already envisioned himself failing. He had programmed himself for failure and then when he went to try, reality conformed to his subconscious or unconscious belief. People end up doing what they think. Their subconscious mind accepts their thoughts as true and accurate.

So be very mindful about your thoughts, because you end up becoming what you think. Use your mind positively. The great philosopher Ralph Waldo Emerson remarked, "The ancestor of every action is a thought." Because this is true, when a negative thought is created by you and put into your mind, the action (the subject and offspring of the thought) is more likely to become a reality.

By changing the inner thoughts of our minds, we can change the outer aspect of our lives.

"The power to create

your future is already

in your hands."

- Dr Tayo Adeyemi

YOUR ATTITUDE
WILL DETERMINE
YOUR ALTITUDE

Your approach, mind-set and stance will determine how you come out of any situation. Whenever you are faced with a difficult situation, the way you respond affects the end result of the situation. If you can stay calm in a storm you might stand a better chance of surviving it. On the other hand, if you panic, you could lose concentration and the willpower to plan your way out of the situation.

No wonder employers seek to recruit people who can

stay calm under pressure. After they are recruited, employees don't always get advance warning about when to expect pressure, but when it comes, the best way out is to be calm and think of the best solution in view of the situation.

What seems nasty, painful, or even evil can become a source of beauty, joy and strength, if faced with an open mind. Every moment can turn out to be a golden one for someone who has the ability to recognise it as such. Whenever you are faced with a difficult situation, see it as an opportunity and approach it with the aim of having a positive outcome. Your attitude is the "single string" that can keep you going or cripple your progress. It can fuel your fire or hinder your hope. No valley is too deep, no mountain too high, barrier too tall, dream too extreme or challenge too great for someone with the right attitude.

DON'T REST ON THE RUNG OF THE LADDER

The rung of a ladder is designed to be a step to propel you to another level. Whatever ladder you climb, don't rest for too long on any rung of the ladder. Whether it is the property ladder, career ladder, or the ladder of life, you should continually expect to move upward, get better, and improve on your last performance.

Whatever level of achievements you have attained, you must remember – the best is yet to come. Don't allow your past achievements to stifle your creativity. There is always room for improvement.

This brings to mind the story of two men who went fishing. One was an experienced fisherman and the other wasn't. Every time the experienced fisherman caught a big fish, he put it in his chest to keep it fresh. Whenever the inexperienced fisherman caught a big fish, he threw it back.

The experienced fisherman watched this go on all day and finally got tired of seeing this man waste good fish. "Why do you keep throwing back all the big fish you catch?" he asked. The inexperienced fisherman replied, "I only have a small frying pan."

Sometimes, we throw back the big plans, big dreams, big jobs and big opportunities that come our way because we cannot see beyond our present circumstances.

See your present circumstances as the rung of a ladder; it is not your destination, but only a stepping stone or spring board that propels you to the next level.

DON'T GIVE UP

Your attitude towards disappointments will affect how you come out of it. Just like it did to Tony Barton, a first time novelist who sent out his manuscript and got 121 rejections. Tony's tenacity made him send it out one more time, and he got his first "Yes". *Indoor Games for the Home Alone* went on to sell more than one million copies.

In 1962, Decca Records wouldn't give the Beatles a recording contract, but the Beatles did not give up and that disappointment did not deter them from making a major impact in the music business.

Most job seekers will tell you, they don't often get a job offer after their first application; it often takes more than one application to secure an employment. People who work in sales and marketing will tell you that it takes endurance, patience and tenacity to close good deals. That's why you must not give up when you are confronted by obstacles.

AGE CONCERN

Do you worry about your advancing age and let it stop you leading a quality life? You may be interested to learn that Ray Kroc was fifty-two when he bought the Mc-Donald brothers' hamburger stand. If you think that was something, how about Colonel Sanders who began his worldwide chain of restaurants when he was in his mid-sixties? Kentucky Fried Chicken (KFC) was the brain child of a retired gentleman!

If you are planning your retirement, the biggest mistake you can make would be to sit down at home and watch television all day. Instead, consider how to enjoy your retirement. Think about the things you've always wanted to do that you couldn't do, and get on with it. Because if you don't, you'll soon find out that boredom is more tiring than hard work.

DON'T DESPISE DAYS OF SMALL BEGINNINGS

Most great things started small. Most people you might think of as achievers or successful mavericks started out small in their field of endeavour. If you are at the bottom of your league don't get discouraged. If you are not commanding attention or making a huge impact at the start of your mission, don't be disheartened.

Tommy Hilfiger, the American designer, started his business by selling jeans from the trunk of his car. Hewlett Packard started his business in a garage, just like Henry Ford started his Ford Motor Company. Dell Computers started right in the classroom. Anita Roddick's Body Shop started in her living room. It doesn't matter how you started. Though your beginning may be small, you don't have to end up small.

Don't get discouraged about teething problems in a project. Humble beginnings can help shape the way you approach your future. If you are determined, you can end up in triumph.

REJECTION DOES NOT MEAN YOU ARE NOT GOOD ENOUGH

It doesn't matter how many hindrances you face. Tenacity and relentless efforts often lead to a positive outcome. If you give up too soon you may not achieve your desired goals. Persistence and continued efforts can help you fulfill your dreams as it has countless other people around the world.

Remember, rejection does not always mean that you are not good enough. If you have a positive attitude, you will always win. Let a positive attitude propel you to victory too.

IF YOU ARE IN A HOLE, STOP DIGGING

You are the person responsible for saving yourself from your circumstances. If you find yourself in a hole, don't try to dig your way out of it or you will end up in a deeper hole. If you find yourself in a hole, stop digging.

It doesn't matter if you are a laid back person or a person of action. You will have your share of challenges in life. You are bound to make some mistakes and face disappointments associated with being a person of action, but don't make matters worse for yourself. Let your actions bring you out of the situation rather than pushing you deeper into the problem.

If you find yourself in a financial hole, before you go and borrow more in order to help relieve your debt, think very carefully about this: There are two logical ways out of debt; minimising your expenditure, or maximising your income. Getting into more debt may temporarily give you a respite, but ultimately, you are increasing your debt.

Likewise, if you have a health, weight or diet problem, avoid the food and lifestyle that contributes to the problem. Doing nothing about your problem will not make it disappear. Whatever you do or don't do, don't make your situation worse. If you are in a hole, stop digging.

DON'T SIT ON THE FENCE

You seldom change things by doing nothing. If you want to change situations, don't sit on the fence; make a quality decision. It is not enough to know that you need to change your situation. It is not enough to know that it is time to move forward in your career or in any area of your life. You must take the next step – Make it happen.

Have you ever met people who know what they need but would not just do anything about it? You seldom get healed by knowing that an aspirin or paracetamol tablet could cure your migraine. The healing comes when you actually consume the medicine. It does not sound logical to know what you need to do to get out of a problem, and you refuse or fail to do it.

Indecision cripples. It hinders you from making progress. This is probably why Nike's slogan is "Just Do It." Get that education, go search for that job, take that driving lesson, stop procrastinating, don't sit on the fence; Make it happen!

BOUNCE BACK

After a crisis it is often tough to maintain a positive mental attitude. Sometimes you feel that you should have listened to those who advised caution or inaction. When you experience a setback, you'll sometimes hear "I told you so" echoing in your mind.

In addition to the reprimand from your conscience, you might also hear the criticism of people around you. These are the important moments of decision. Instead of accepting all this torture, become determined to change the situation. It doesn't really matter how much time, talent or money may have been wasted. If you want to make progress, stop blaming yourself and bounce back. It is a choice you have to make. How you decide to react in these challenging defining moments will ultimately make all the difference.

IT'S A NEW DAY

You must also develop the inner fortitude and peace of mind to deal with misfortunes within or outside your control: a failed project, unsuccessful business venture, a sick child, bereavement, abandonment or rejection by a loved one, crime, personal illnesses or natural disasters. Things may feel so devastating that you can't rationally put them into perspective. You must remember that you cannot do anything about your past, but you can do something about your future. Yesterday is gone, tomorrow is ahead, and today is all you have. Start today to do something about your tomorrow.

Make It Happen

It doesn't matter what circumstances you face, your attitude will always determine your altitude.

Positive anyting is better

than negative nothing.

Nothing can stop someone
with the right mental
attitude from achieving
his or her goal.

GOAL KEEPER

Would you get into a bus without a destination in mind or get off at any bus stop you picked at random? Would you get on board a taxi and tell the cab driver, "drive anywhere?" Would you wander into the first train that comes to your platform at the train station without checking the Information Board? Would you book a flight to a strange country without a purpose for your visit? Of course not! No one in their right mind would do such things, yet it is amazing to see how unfocused we can be about the biggest asset we possess – our lives.

You must have a precise, exact, streamlined, and specific goal for your life. Goal Keeping helps you to be focused and enables you to harness your determination to succeed. It also helps you to be prepared for the future. A farmer does not wait for the harvest season before he starts to prepare. He plans for both his planting and harvesting season long in advance. Those who anticipate the next season make things happen.

When faced with a choice of living for today or living for tomorrow... choose tomorrow. Immature people always want instant gratification and choose to enjoy today at the expense of tomorrow. Just as people with poverty mentality have an insatiable desire for goods which they really cannot afford, demonstrated by their debt-ridden 'buy today and pay tomorrow' lifestyle, rich people are future-oriented and save for the rainy days ahead. It's better to put money aside for future use than to borrow from your future. This is achievable if you have a financial goal.

WHO OR WHAT IS A GOAL KEEPER?

In many team sports, the Goal Keeper is the person charged with directly defending the goal and preventing the opposite team from scoring. In ice hockey, the Goal Keeper is known as a goaltender. A Goal Keeper looks out for potential threats and is always ready to dive to parry an opponent's shots from his goal area.

It might interest you to know that Goal Keeper is also the designation of a Dutch CIWS (close-in weapon system) naval shipboard weapon system for detecting and destroying incoming anti-ship missiles and enemy aircraft. In this case the Goal Keeper defends a ship against incoming missiles and ballistic shells. The system consists of an auto-cannon and advanced radar which tracks incoming fire, determines its trajectory, then aims the cannon and fires in a matter of seconds. The system is fully automatic, needing no human input once activated. The kinetic energy of the 30mm rounds is sufficient to destroy any missile or shell. The system can also be deployed to protect airfields.

Just as in football or CIWS, a Goal Keeper is a custodian tasked with warding off all potential threats to the fulfilment of an ambition, objective or aspiration. You should have a goal, aim or objective towards which your endeavours are directed and which you would guard diligently.

Think about the next few years. Where will you be in five or ten years? Go further; think of yourself in old age. Do you have a goal to be successful? Do you have a goal for your family, career or business? If you want to look back with a smile and congratulate yourself for your efforts or if you want your golden years to be filled with fond memories and not with deep regrets, you should have a goal which you will keep and tend in order to ensure that your vision becomes a reality.

Goal setting gives you control over the direction of your life's journey. Goal setting is personal power. Many are careless about their future, believing in the old song "Que sera sera, whatever will be will be." But if you set goals and assume control of your own life; "whatever will be" will depend on you rather than on others.

IF YOU FAIL TO PLAN, YOU'VE PLANNED TO FAIL

A goal without a plan is just a wish. It is important that you break your goals down into little objectives and do-able tasks. You may choose to call this your action plan. You need a list or a plan of actions which will enable you to achieve your goals.

Most people wish to be successful but have no plan for success. If you fail to plan, it means you have planned to fail. If you don't have a plan for your daily activities at work you could be very busy yet ineffective.

The actions you take translate your goals from your paper or computer into reality. Think about the right course of action and the appropriate strategy for your goal. Let your goals (the big picture) be broken down into objectives (the small pictures). These will become daily things-to-do. Your plans develop momentum and they will help to steer you towards your goals. You can only achieve your goals through an Action Plan.

Planning helps you to select your opportunities. If you are not selective about opportunities that come your way, you will accept every offer, dissipate your energy and waste your resources. Planning gives you something to aim for.

Let's say that you would love to start your own business / change jobs or career / start a family / buy a house or car / invest in your personal development... hopefully, not all at the same time. It is important that you start planning to achieve your goals because to be successful, you must carefully plan your work, and then work your plan into action.

HAVE REALISTIC PLANS

Your plans should be challenging but realistic and achievable. Plans that are too easy or too hard can negatively affect your motivation. Your plans should not be blurry, half-baked or fuzzy. Living a deliberate life requires being focused because the life you're living today is a product of the choices you made yesterday.

The more precise, exact, streamlined, and specific you are about where you're going the more powerful your life will be. It is no use planning to build a castle in the air, unless you have the resources. Always match your plan with your resources, other wise your plan would be unrealistic.

WRITE DOWN YOUR PLAN

When you decide on the changes you want to make in your life and begin to define your plans, write them down. Many successful people regard this as a critical step. If you write it down, you are taking that first small step toward accomplishing it. It may seem to be a little thing, quite inconsequential in the grand scheme of things but writing down your goals and plans is of the utmost importance.

It's like starting with 20 and then breaking it down: 20 = 10 + 7 + 3. First comes the big picture, then the bits that make the big picture complete. Make up your mind about your goal, then decide the steps or plan (how and when) you will achieve it.

Write it down so that you can revisit it and let your written plans remind and motivate you to take the necessary actions, only then will you be on the road to making something positive happen.

CONCRETE GOALS AND FLEXIBLE PLANS

Circumstances may cause interruptions and delays, but never lose sight of your goal. Prepare yourself in every way you can by increasing your knowledge and adding to your experience, so that you can make the most of every opportunity when it occurs. If it becomes obvious that your goals cannot be reached through the original plan, don't adjust the goals, adjust the action plan.

Set your goal in concrete or cast it in iron, but let your plans be written on paper or scribbled on sand. Be defiant about your goals but less rigid about your plans. Your plans may change depending on your circumstances but let all the changes culminate into helping you achieve your goals.

TYPES OF GOALS

Look at the following life categories. Then decide what goals and plans fit where you are now in your life and the direction you'd like your journey to take.

INVESTMENT GOALS

Investment goals demand that you sacrifice today for tomorrow. That's why you must avoid the temptation of "Buy now, pay later." This would mean you were borrowing from rather than investing in your future.

Are you preparing for a long retirement? Have you taken the time to understand the benefits of your pension and other retirement plans? In what industries do you have specialized knowledge that you can put to profitable investment use? Do you know successful market investors whose advice and strategies you can adopt?

■ CAREER GOALS

Career goals place you in a position to earn enough money to have all the material possessions and time that you want for yourself. Can you take a second job or accept overtime? Can you go back to college to improve your career prospects? Can you invest in your personal development so that you can become such a valuable employee that your company will fear losing you? Can you start your own business?

■ RELAXATION GOALS

An adage says "All work and no play makes Jack a dull boy". Do you have plans for your relaxation time? How do you relax? Do you read books? Can you go to the cinema, concerts or gallery shows? Are you savouring fine foods and wines? Do you listen to great music? Start thinking creatively of ways of filling your life with beauty and let nothing stop you from living well… and remember to do so within your means.

FAMILY GOALS

Family goals allow you to share and to enjoy life with a kindred spirit or partner and to pass on all your best qualities to a new generation. How can you be a better husband, wife, parent, aunt or uncle? Can you write a note or e-mail? Call or visit a lonely family member?

SPIRITUAL GOALS

Spiritual goals give you an opportunity to look at the big picture. What is your relationship with God? What is your responsibility to the environment and to your fellow human being? What do you intend to leave as your legacy? How will your one life have made a difference to humanity?

PHYSICAL GOALS

Physical goals challenge you to be as fit and healthy as possible. You can't change genetics or avoid all accidents but you don't have to waddle through life either. Are you exercising, watching your weight and getting enough sleep? Physical exercise can also help you to reduce stress and align your priorities. Have you chosen a life sport? Jogging for example?

COMMUNITY SERVICE GOALS

Community service goals give you the opportunity to give something back to your community. Can you volunteer to work for a worthwhile local cause? Can you donate money? Can you run in a race to raise money for those in need? Can you run for a political office? Former British Prime Minister, Winston Churchill, said, "We make a living by what we get. We make a life by what we give."

▯ *INTELLECTUAL GOALS*

Intellectual goals encourage you to commit to a life of curiosity and self-education. Books, magazines, talks, speeches, seminars, courses and the entire world of the internet are amongst your resources. This new millennium presents opportunities for unparalleled academic advancement. How will you improve on your intelligence? If you want to be a good leader you should be a good reader because leaders are readers.

▯ *OTHER GOALS*

Do you have any other personal goals? Make a wish without worrying about your abilities, experiences or assets. What would you be able to do? How much money would you have? What would you create? Where would you live? What sort of home would you have? Would you buy, rent or build a house? Where would you like to visit? Would you own a pet or a luxury car? Let your goals reflect the outcomes that you desire.

WHAT YOU WANT WILL AFFECT HOW YOU PLAN

As you create your goals and plans, consider these words of wisdom:

If you are planning for one year, grow rice.
If you are planning for 20 years, grow trees.
If you are planning for centuries, grow individuals.

The size of your plans is determined by the size of your goals. If you are planning to build a shed in a garden or to assemble a flat packed filing cabinet, all you need are a little schematic, some screws and a screwdriver.

But if your goal is to build a house, you will need much more than that. You will need a building plan, surveyor, risk assessment, and plans for the electrical installations, plumbing, bricklaying and machinery. You'll also need to plan to recruit an architect, building contractors and so on. The size of your plan and the resources required will depend on the size and nature of your goal.

Write your vision.

Make it clear

so that whoever reads it will understand it.

Habits change

into character.

CHANGE YOUR BAD HABITS

All habits whether good or bad are learned and can be unlearned. Habits are ingrained regular behavioural patterns or repetitive unconscious actions.

Bad habits may originally seem harmless, but they can eventually cause stress, tension and anxiety. For example, it may be something you want to start doing (like exercising) or something you want to stop doing (like eating the wrong food at the wrong time). It doesn't matter what it is or how long you've had the habit. It can be changed if you believe you can do it, and if you have the desire, determination, practical skills and knowledge of how to change it.

WHY DO BAD HABITS HAVE SUCH A TIGHT GRIP ON US?

A teacher once illustrated the power of bad habits to her students in the following manner. She took a roll of thread and wrapped it one time around a student's wrists that were placed together. "This represents the power of doing something one time," she explained. "Can you break the thread?"

The student easily did so. Then the teacher wrapped the thread many times around the wrists and repeated the challenge to break them. Despite real effort, the thread was too strong to be broken. "This is the power of repeated actions, or habits," she explained.

Habits have such a tight grip on us because they are repeated ingrained behavioural patterns. If you want to break a bad habit you must recognise that it has the upper hand on you, so you must be deliberate and persistent in your approach. Interestingly, many bad habits have honourable roots. They start as an effort to accomplish something positive. Swearing, for example, can begin as an attempt to communicate dissatisfaction and disagreement. But when you develop the reputation of one who can generally be found "swearing like a light bulb," any notions about your pure intentions quickly evaporate.

Unfortunately bad habits have a way of creeping up on us. What started out as occasional cigarettes ends up as life threatening lung cancer. What started out as a bar of chocolate each time you wanted to give yourself a treat ends up as 15 pounds of unwanted body weight. An occasional white lie becomes a complex chain of untruths.

POOR FUTURE ORIENTATION LEADS TO BAD HABITS

Bad habits can be caused by a preference for instant gratification otherwise known as... poor future orientation. The decision making process that sustains bad habits focuses on the present rather than the future. That's why people with poor future orientation often have a more difficult struggle with bad habits.

Have you noticed that people who cannot handle delayed gratification struggle with poor financial habits? Such people feel they must have whatever they feel like having right now and at any cost. They will not wait until they are able to afford it.

Most habitual smokers do so because of the need for instant gratification. They light up a cigarette after a good meal or to seek relief from the effects of a stressful day. Most smokers know the consequences but always hope to be the few lucky ones who will escape lung cancer. However, after many years of smoking, an X-ray result of their cancer-ridden lungs often forces such smokers to begin to think of a bleak future as the inevitable outcome if they continue smoking. This contrasts quite sharply with their previous disposition towards instant gratification.

KNOW YOUR BAD HABITS

What habit do you want to change that will make your life better? Take a minute or two to think about it and write it down. Also make a list of what it is costing you every day, to continue with that habit.

Now, take a few minutes to think about the cost of not changing that habit. You might ask yourself, "Where will I be in three, five, or ten years, if I don't make that change?" Use your imagination. A written record can serve as a great reminder later on, when your motivation slips.

Some bad habits are such a part of our daily lives that it's easy to forget we have them. Other bad habits you may want to change could range from poor time management, allowing paperwork to pile sky high on your desk, drug abuse or alcoholism.

Some habits may be induced by psychological disorders such as Obsessive Compulsive Disorder (OCD) or paranoia. Always seek medical support in breaking free of these underlying causes and the bad habits they have engendered.

JUMPSTART YOUR NEW YEAR RESOLUTIONS

Many people wait until 1st January before they initiate a change towards a better life. Many even endure several months to put off giving up a bad habit until 1st of January. But you don't have to wait until 1st of January to give up a harmful, sinful or unfruitful way of life. Jumpstart your New Year resolution, today!

Don't wait until New Year's Eve before you conduct a review of how you've spent the current year. Carry out your evaluation today, and begin to plan what you will do this year and not do next year. If you are really serious about giving up your bad habits, don't wait until the last few minutes of New Year's Eve. Initiate the change today.

Start making the necessary plans. Take action to make your vision come to fruition. That's how to jumpstart your New Year resolution.

HOW TO CHANGE YOUR BAD HABITS

1.   LET THE TRUTH PREVAIL

The first step to breaking a bad habit is to accept that you have a bad habit. Let the truth prevail. A clinical psychologist once wrote about a study involving participants who had failed to lose weight on 20 or more diets and weight-loss programs. The participants insisted that the reason for their failure was genetic, because they ate very little and still couldn't lose weight. When researchers carefully recorded participants' eating habits 24 hours a day, they found that they were eating twice as much as they claimed. These people simply had a weak awareness of their behaviour, and this lack of insight perpetuated their bad habits.

If you don't know and refuse to accept that you have a bad habit it is almost impossible to change it. Habits gradually blend in with our everyday behaviour, becoming almost automatic. When this happens, they follow us wherever we go. Lack of awareness allows habits to grow, while awareness helps us escape our habits.

2.   MOTIVATION

Make a list of the wonderful advantages you'll enjoy if you do change your habits. Take a couple of minutes to think about the benefits of changing the habits and try to come up with at least five things. What will your life be like in the next one or two years if you change those habits? This should motivate you to change them.

3.   REPLACE BAD HABITS WITH GOOD ONES

For example, if you must snack after dinner, fill your fridge with healthy food like fruits rather than chocolates and cakes. If you have a habit of watching television programmes or doing things that stifle your creativity, cultivate the habit of reading books and magazines or be selective about the TV programmes you watch.

4.   CHANGE YOUR ENVIRONMENT

Indeed, one of the most powerful methods to breaking a bad habit is to place yourself in an environment that encourages your new good habit.

If you are a student and there is no quiet place to study at home, change your study environment. Do your homework and study at the library instead. Some people find a very quite place counter-productive when they want to concentrate on a job or study. For such people, playing music or radio while they work may be helpful.

Bad habits could also evolve from your upbringing. For example – disorganisation is a combination of habits and traits. Traits are inborn, whereas habits are acquired.

It's true that many people who are disorganised were "brought up that way," but often the problem is compounded by the fact that few people are taught basic organising skills either at home or at school. It is certainly possible to learn these skills, and people who make an ongoing effort can change their habits and become more organised.

5. *BREAK THE CHAIN EARLY WITH WARNING SIGNS*

If you break the chain early you can avoid the unwanted behaviours. Carefully placed warning signs can help you change your bad habits. If you want to avoid watching TV for hours, set your mobile phone or alarm clock to warn you after one hour. If you want to avoid eating junk food, don't stock up your fridge with junk food and paste a good-food-chart on your fridge. Let it warn you and guide your eating habits.

6. *FACILITATE THE GOOD HABITS*

If you go straight to the gym before going home after work, you may succeed in maintaining a regular exercise routine. But if you go home first, the sight of your comfortable sofa in front of the TV may mean a battle with your willpower, and end up in surrender.

Changing a bad habit, and improving your life, takes commitment and facilitation. Get started today by committing to change your bad habit, gradually. Then encourage your-self, avoid distractions, stay focused and reward yourself for achieving positive results.

Don't do whatever you want

just because you can.

If you don't set boundaries for yourself,

someone will do it for you.

He who won't be

counselled can't be helped.

CULTIVATE GOOD RELATIONSHIPS

Relationships will make or break you. Positive relationships will enhance your vision and negative relationships will be detrimental to the fulfilment of your vision. You cannot achieve all your goals all by yourself; you need the involvement of others. In the business sector, firms increasingly search for constructive relations with their clients and other firms which will ultimately offer them a competitive edge.

NO ONE IS AN ISLAND

Alexander Graham Bell said "Great discoveries and improvements invariably involve the cooperation of many minds" and there is an African proverb that says "you cannot clap with just one hand." The support, encouragement, motivation, knowledge and information you get from other people will help you to achieve your goals.

It is a common saying that "no man is an island." All these idiomatic expressions seem to point towards one direction; you seldom become victorious alone. It is a common belief among managers that everything rises and falls on leadership, but I will add "a leader is jobless without a follower".

If you want to achieve a positive result in any endeavour, look for someone or people who will propel you to make progress.

BEWARE OF FIRE FIGHTERS

If you are passionate about your dream, beware of people who could kill the dream. If you are "on fire" about an idea and approach people about it, you could face one of two types of people: People with buckets full of water or people with buckets full of petrol. Those with water will quench your dreams and those with petrol will fuel them.

If you have a dream or vision, don't tell pessimistic people. Whatever you want to achieve, don't ask the wrong people. They may tell you, "No." They may give you every excuse in the book. They may give you every reason for failure. Such people could tell you the downside of any decision you want to make.

If you have respect for them it will be very easy for you to rationalise and take comfort in their answers, especially if you respect them for their past achievements. Or perhaps they are older than you so you think they should have more experience.

About one hundred years ago Mark Twain saw this happening when he said, "Keep away from people who try to belittle your ambitions. Small people always do that, but the really great make you feel that you, too, can become great."

This sentiment is shared by American Children's Activist Marian Wright Edelman, "No person has the right to rain on your dreams." The famous American broadcaster David Brinkley notes, "A successful man is one who can build a firm foundation with the bricks that others throw at him." And Ralph Waldo Emerson said, "Whatever course you decide upon, there is always someone to tell you that you are wrong."

MENTORING

One of the most interesting developments in recent years has been the growth of mentoring for very senior executives. This is often done through external mentors, although some organisations have experimented with peer mentoring schemes especially at director level. Mentoring at this level has a somewhat different role. There is less emphasis on application of learning and more on being a mixture of critical friend and a sounding board.

This level of helping activity is particularly prone to confusion between coaching and mentoring. A mentor is an experienced, trusted adviser or guide. In most cases, mentors have "been there, seen it and done it." On the other hand, a coach does not necessarily have to have the exact experience. Most national football coaches never played football for their national teams.

BENCHMARKING

Benchmarking involves selecting a demonstrated standard of products, services, costs, or practices that represent the very best performance for processes or activities very similar to your own. The idea is to develop a target at which to shoot and then develop a standard or benchmark against which to compare your performance.

The following are some suggested steps for developing benchmarks:

1   Determine what to benchmark.
2   Form a benchmark team.
3   Identify benchmarking partners.
4   Collect and analyse benchmarking information.
5   Take action to match or exceed the benchmark.

In an ideal situation, you will find one or more people or organisations succeeding in your area of interest that you admire and would like to study the secrets of their success. Then you compare yourself (benchmark yourself) against them. The individual or organisation need not be in your industry or chosen field of endeavour. Benchmarks often take the form of "best practices" found in other individuals or organisations. It is better to benchmark what has been tried, tested and true, than to embark on an innovative and precarious idea.

NETWORKS AND CONNECTIONS

As you think about entrepreneurial opportunities, don't forget any networks or connections that may give you an advantage in your endeavours.

Does your uncle or your neighbour or your sister-in-law

or a former classmate have connections to assist your project? Somebody you know probably knows somebody who would be willing to give you special assistance because of a personal contact. Build positive networks. Associate with people who are committed to self-improvement and helping others. You can go far by yourself and even further with the help of other people.

Walt Disney said, "All you've got to do is open up to your own ignorance honestly, and you'll find people who are eager to fill your head with information." If you want to make things happen for you, you must be willing to seek the support of others. Don't be too arrogant to seek help and don't be so shy you suffer in silence. If you are an inquisitive person you will seek, and if you seek you will find.

UNDERSTAND THE "LAW OF RECOGNITION"

What you don't recognise will eventually leave you. You seldom greet people you don't recognise, at least not as enthusiastically as the people you do recognise. In the same vein, organisations often give more attention and recognition to their most valued customers.

Look for instances of the 80/20 rule. It pops up a lot. For example, the 80/20 rule says that 80% of your business will come from 20% of your customers. It continues that 80% of your profits will come from 20% of your products.

Recognise people who are smarter, hard working or more ambitious than you are. Achievers are constantly on the lookout for outstanding performers. If you own a hair-dressing saloon and find an unemployed hairdresser who is more skilful than you or other members of your staff, you may want to encourage him or her to work for you. If you are an entrepreneur, one question you should consid-er is: are your competitors good enough to hire, take over or join in a merger? Can you name your most important customers? Are you doing anything special for them? Are you at least in regular communication with them? If not, you are creating an opportunity for your competitors.

ENCOURAGE DIALOGUE IN YOUR ORGANISATION

Listen to people who have ideas for improvement even if those ideas are in conflict with your own. It is very easy to surround yourself with deceptive people who take no risks in always agreeing with your "brilliant thoughts." This gets you nowhere. It is much more productive to en-gage in honest dialogue and debate with intelligent people who are not only unafraid but also encouraged to offer their opinions.

If you really want to make progress at work you should borrow a leaf from John Maxwell who says, "the more successful you become, the more you have to look at people and say; be honest with me, be realistic with me and tell me what you think I need to work on. Otherwise, people start telling you only what they think you want to hear, which keeps you from getting good, honest feedback that you need."

GOOD RELATIONSHIPS ARE VITAL FOR BUSINESS

To do good business you need a quick mind, a head for figures, and many other qualities. But above all, you need the ability to build good relationships. It is human nature to desire to be liked, valued and respected: If you want to succeed in the business arena, you must cultivate good relationships. Show your clients or customers that you like, value and respect them.

Social investments often yield dividends for businesses. Social investment is different from networking as it requires a level of proactive concern for others. You may need to make sustained and repeated contact with your clients. This may be done by phone, fax, email, teleconference or letter writing. Whichever way you choose, keep in touch with them on a regular basis.

People don't care how much you know until they know how much you care. Successful deal-making and successful business depends on keen observation and understanding of the interests and characteristics of your clients. People show interest in those who care about them. They trust those they know and help those whom they know well. This is why relationships are vital for business.

LEARN TO DELEGATE

You may get a lot done but you can accomplish more when others help. Whether you are leading your family, company or team, you must be able to delegate assignments. Delegating means to pass responsibility to others. Delegating helps you concentrate on what you do best and allows you to think, plan and improve organisational efficiency. Delegate the tasks that are most cost and time effective for others to do for you. Also, delegate those tasks that other people can do better than you.

Working with someone with superior talents

does not diminish your talents.

Don't settle for instant

gratification when you can

settle for a lifetime of

significance.

INTEGRITY AND INTENSITY

Integrity and intensity are two words that will help you make things happen. If you want to stand the test of time in any endeavour, you must be someone with integrity and intensity. Integrity is who you are and intensity is what you do.

INTEGRITY

Integrity comes from the root word "integer." This means a unit, or all one. It means that your word and your actions are one. It means living a life that does not carry double standards.

Integrity refers to the character of a product, person or thing. A product or service could maintain its integrity as long as it continues to meet the need and satisfaction of its customers. An employee maintains his or her integrity as long as he/she is not in breach of trust.

The patronage of a product or service is based on trust. People will buy or use your product or service because they trust you. If you betray their trust by selling or supplying a poor quality product it will be difficult to regain.

In any business your word is your honour. It is your bond and it becomes synonymous with your name. If you make a promise, you should endeavour to keep it, because your word is your equity. When you fail morally or in character people may forgive you but they are not obliged to trust you. Trust is something you earn, if you lose it, it is often hard to retrieve.

I.   YOUR WORD

Some people will not buy a product again because they were disappointed the last time they did. When people have a bad experience of any product or service they do not keep it to themselves. They often tell others who also relay the bad news to others. Bad news travel faster than good news. That is why you must honour your word whether it is given orally or in writing, on a leaflet or on the packaging of your product.

The number one cause of children's resentment to their parents is broken promises. Likewise, it is the major cause of dissatisfaction with a product or service.

2. *BAD DECISIONS*

One thing that can affect your integrity is the quality of your decisions. You make decisions based on the information you have. Bad information often leads to bad decisions. That's why you must carefully evaluate the credibility and reliability of your source of information before you utilise it, because ultimately, your integrity is on the line.

INTENSITY

The attention, tenacity and concentration you give to a project will determine how far you go with it. If you really want to make things happen, you must be willing to give it all it takes. You must be prepared to go all the way. This is intensity.

The term intensity is often used, and is most times confused with the term work, or volume of work. So misused is the term that a body builder might remark, "Man, my workout lasted two hours - it was intense" or "I did 30 sets for biceps, it was so intense." Or a student might say, "My study time was so intense last night – I studied all night."

The sad reality is that many people use the term intensity to mean hard work. As you will find in the other chapters of this book, hard work is good but smart work is better. So where does intensity come into the equation? Intensity is about frequency and consistency.

Going back to the body builder and the student mentioned above, it is counter productive if a bodybuilder erroneously increases the amount of weight he or she carries but decreases the distance over which he or she goes.

Likewise, someone who has not done any physical exercise for a long time may go to the gym to lift heavy weights in a quest for intensity, hoping to achieve their goal on their first attempt. The key is gradual and consistent exercise rather than forceful one-off exercise.

For the student, consistent study time on a daily basis will be helpful and lead to more success than one sleepless night of concentrated study.

It should also be noted that while intensity is not a measure of work done, it is a measure of the effort applied while doing that work. Intensity as it applies to work is not a measure of work done but the time over which the work is done.

Someone once said, "It's not what you do that counts, but how much love and passion you put to it." If you are passionate about what you do, you will not count how much time and effort you put into it. This brings to mind another proverb that says, "Those who do the things that count don't count the things they do."

STAY FOCUSED

If you want to intensify the things you do, aim to stay focused. One of the reasons why most people find it difficult to fulfil their vision and make their dreams become reality is their inability to stay focused.

Some people start off each year with a New Year resolution but within a few months get sidetracked. Likewise, at the beginning of training programmes, classes are often full but attendance quickly drops. Another example is the people who earmark time and money for driving lessons. For many, within a short time, those resources have been diverted into other activities to the detriment of their ambition to learn how to drive.

One of the challenges for most people is to stay focused on a major project or target. During the course of a project, unexpected matters tend to surface that can divert their attention. This often makes it difficult for many to stay purposeful or resolute in the pursuit of their mission.

If you are on a mission it does not matter how many distractions show up to hinder your progress... Don't stop. Keep on going. It does not matter how slowly you go, as long as you do not stop.

These four suggestions can help you remain focused on reaching your targets:

1.   *KEEP YOUR EYE ON THE GOAL*
Isn't it remarkable that children can be on their best behaviour when they look forward to going on a trip or are promised a treat? A child will happily wake up unaided at 5.00 am on the morning of an exciting trip or event.

Likewise, a man with a 52 inch waistline can endure the difficult tasks necessary to lose weight and reduce his waist size in order to impress a new girlfriend; a larger lady can tolerate the pressure of losing weight to fit into a smaller wedding gown; a student may undergo six or more years of medical school to become a medical doctor; an athlete may endure four years of hard training motivated by the dream of an Olympic medal. These people stay focused because of the goal at stake.

Keeping your eye on the potential benefits of an endeavour will motivate you to give it what it takes to achieve the goal. If you have the end in mind, you will endure the process by keeping your eye on the goal.

2. *IF YOU WANT TO LEAD AN ORCHESTRA, TURN YOUR BACK ON THE CROWD*

One day my wife was helping Peter, my eight year old son, with his homework. I noticed that the television was switched on and every few minutes Peter would look away to catch a glimpse of the TV.

I suggested that they could achieve better results if they turned off the TV or relocated to another room in the house. Within a few minutes, they had made tremendous progress with the homework. Your key to success can be as simple as that... If you want to stay focused remove the distraction.

If you want a positive outcome in any endeavour you must be focused, and not allow people or things to distract your attention. That is why conductors often face the orchestra with their backs to the crowd.

You must make a solitary decision to be focused on your mission. Your mission may not be accomplished if you drift along with the crowd or pay attention to their responses. You must be willing to stand alone.

Obstacles may come your way, but you must be willing to overcome them. Negotiate around corners, if you must. Leap over hurdles, if you have to. Climb mountains or hop down valleys, if necessary. Whatever you do, don't let these distractions deter you from keeping your focus.

3.   *URGENT, IMPORTANT AND CRISIS*

Your daily work can be divided into three main types; Urgent, Important and Crisis. Many times at work, you'll find many urgent things calling for your attention. Most of the time, these urgent things are not important. At other times, important matters call for your attention but they are not urgent so you may postpone them or procrastinate.

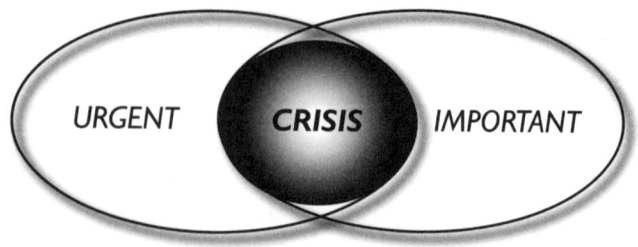

But if you keep responding to urgent calls for your time and energy, you will leave the important things undone. This might then lead to a crisis situation when something becomes both urgent and important at the same time. The key is to stay focused on important things to help minimise or avoid crisis situations.

4.   CONSISTENCY

Another important key if you want to remain focused is consistency. Most people can carry out a short term, one or two day project but projects that demand weeks, months and years are a challenge to many people. Any worthwhile or challenging goal requires persistent and sustained efforts. Take a look at these two proverbs: " A thousand mile journey starts with just one step." "Little drops of water can make a mighty ocean".

The common principle illustrated by the proverbs is the principle of "consistency." A thousand mile journey cannot be accomplished unless you take one step and continue with more steps. Likewise, little drops of water don't make an ocean unless many more follow.

If you are able to pay the price

you can achieve whatever you want.

The starting point

of motion is desire

DESIRE IS THE KEY TO MOTIVATION

Everything that you create or acquire begins with desire. The first part of a journey from the abstract to the concrete is in the arena of the imagination. Here, plans for its conversion are created and organised.

Desire is the key to motivation. Your desire triggers off the determination and commitment to help you pursue your goal unrelentingly. Whatever you want to make happen will start with a desire.

Whatever you desire, you must be prepared to pay the price to enable you attain the success you wish. If you desire any goal, know the benefit of achieving it, believe you can reach it and are prepared to make the commitment that it requires, you can make it happen.

Now let's get back to your desire. What do you want? Have you considered the benefits and cost implications and are you prepared to pay the price? If you've answered yes to these questions, your desire is achievable.

There is no hope of success for the person who does not have a central purpose or definite goal. For example, if you attend an educational institution with the aim of graduating at the end of the academic year, this will affect how you make use of your time. It will influence how you study and the extra-curricular activities you are involved with.

If you simply went to college because your friends or family expected you to, you might end up not graduating. The activities in an educational institution are geared towards attaining a certificate or graduation, not merely to please someone else.

DESIRE DEMYSTIFIED

Desire is the thought that leads to an action. It is an internal state or condition that activates behaviour and gives it direction. It energises and directs goal-oriented behaviour. Desire influences intensity. There is very limited likelihood of success for the person who does not have a desire, central purpose or clearly defined goal to aim for.

Desire provides motivation in life. It is the catalyst or energy that keeps you moving forward toward your goals and the life of your dreams. An internal instinct based on survival, desire helps motivate you to search, acquire, and consume the necessary ingredients for living.

A burning desire is the foundation for productive motivation. Desire stimulates creative thinking. What you want to do and what you can do is limited only by what you can dream or desire.

If you do not have the desire for something, you will not have the motivation to go for it. True desire comes from your heart. Unlike a TV advert or advice which prompts you to choose a product or service to feel fulfilled and happy, true desire is uniquely within you.

This instinct to fulfil desire is an essential part of your thought process. Desire and passion work together. Your passions form a vision in your mind of what you want and think you need to be happy in life. Desire motivates and energises every step you take on your pathway to fulfil these needs.

While desire is the key to motivation, determination and commitment to an unrelenting pursuit of your goal and a commitment to excellence will enable you to attain the success you seek.

If you don't translate your desire into action but translate it into fantasy, it remains wishful thinking. Targets are not achieved by wishing they'll happen but by making them happen.

In summary, to make it happen, start with a desire, translate it into written goals, break these down into "bite size" objectives and, finally, take action matched with wisdom. Nothing just happens.

Nothing can dim the light

which shines from within.

COMING SOON

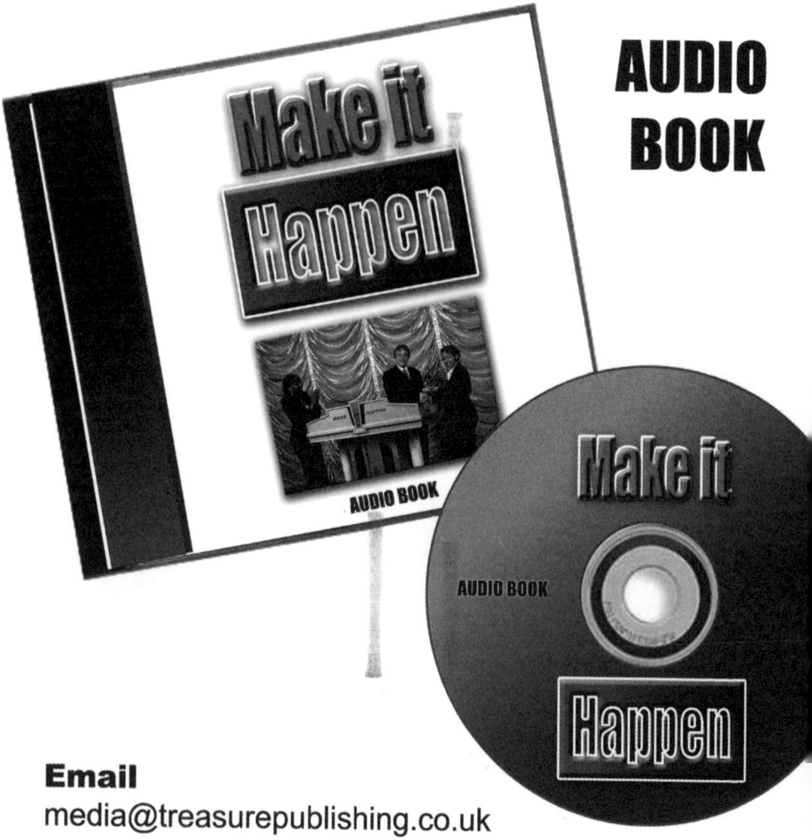

AUDIO BOOK

Make it Happen

AUDIO BOOK

Email
media@treasurepublishing.co.uk

Website
www.treasurepublishing.co.uk
www.socialcaremagazine.com/treasure